NATURE'S LIFE LESSONS

Everyday Truths from Nature

NATURE'S LIFE LESSONS

Everyday Truths from Nature

JIM CARRIER

and

MARC BEKOFF

Illustrations by Marjorie C. Leggitt

Fulcrum Publishing
Golden, Colorado

Library of Congress Cataloging-in-Publication Data

Carrier, Jim.
    Nature's life lessons : everyday truths from nature / Jim Carrier
and Marc Bekoff.

    p.   cm.
    ISBN 1-55591-248-6 (pbk.). — ISBN 1-55591-274-5 (8 copy prepack)
    1. Animals—Humor.   2. Nature—Humor.   I. Bekoff, Marc.
II. Title.
PN 6231.A5C37   1996
818'.5402—dc20   95-49006
                                                    CIP

Printed in the United States of America

0 9 8 7 6 5 4 3 2 1

Fulcrum Publishing
350 Indiana Street, Suite 350
Golden, Colorado 80401-5093
(800) 992-2908

TABLE OF CONTENTS

❧ INTRODUCTION ❧

> **WARNING LABEL:** *This is not a cuddly nature book. What you are about to experience is life in the raw. Do not open if you are faint-of-heart, hypersensitive, a prude, a sexist, a feminist or even especially civilized— unless you also can laugh at yourself.*

    Nature's Life Lessons states in human terms the gritty, sometimes brutal, behavior of plants and animals, including mammals, birds, and fish. In this world there is no such thing as equality or morality, no right or wrong. Survival of the fittest can mean dominance. Perhaps just as often, deceit is employed. To survive, animals may behave in what seems to us selfish ways. This book is not about being politically correct, but it is about being biologically correct.

    Neither is this book anthropomorphic—giving nonhuman animals human attributes. Just the opposite. We start with nonhuman animal behavior, evolved over centuries, and apply it to the human condition. From "lower" forms of life come surprising answers for our socialized lives. Many clichés—the ugly duckling, the pecking order, the crying wolf—are bits of observed truth in every language. Behavior that evolved from the primordial goo is still stuck in our cells. To make this simple to understand we have taken the liberty of using words such as females and girls, males and guys.

Nature's Life Lessons takes off where these familiar clichés end; to find ideas for business people swimming with sharks, for singles on the prowl, for families, lovers, the weak, and the lonely.

Animals want three things—a meal, a family, a safe home—and they have created many different ways to get them. Monogamy, for example, is the exception in many species. Aggression also may be common, but usually not to the point of self destruction. Brutal and thoughtless as some of these behaviors may seem, it's refreshing to know that they evolved without jealousy, anger, hatred, and greed.

There is evidence, too, that altruism, compassion, and learning in animals are signs of early intelligence.

Also, survival of the fittest doesn't necessarily mean that only big and strong animals mate and survive, as is commonly assumed. In many species, smaller and weaker individuals can win mates and territory, too. And, it's important to qualify that in large groups such as mice, monkeys, and ants, not every member behaves the same.

Nature's Life Lessons is a celebration of the infinitely resourceful ways in which nature thrives. We hope in these one-liners you will learn something about the natural world, have fun, and feel connected to your fellow creations. Who knows, they might have something to teach you!

To cool off on a hot day, flap your ears.

(Elephant)

CHAPTER ONE

IT'S A JUNGLE OUT THERE

If confronted by a mugger, show your stripes, swish your tail, and do pushups.

(Yarrow spiny lizard)

Shop at night to avoid long lines.

(Owl)

To be safe at bedtime,
change into darker clothing.

(Coral fish)

When climbing life's ladder, keep an eye on
your behind. There's always someone
ready to bite it.

(Baboon)

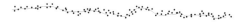

Losing your mind? Grow another.

(Earthworm)

Don't trust humans.

(All species)

In a gathering you can tell who are friends;
they're sharing food.

(Chimpanzee)

All good fliers check maintenance
on their wings before taking off.

(Duck)

A lone wolf may sound romantic,
but a group survives.

(Fish)

To avoid sunburn, roll in the mud.

(Pig)

If you're caught by a robber in an alley,
roll on your back, hum,
and poop in your pants.

(Burying beetle)

Don't ever get between two females.

(Jackal)

If you've been spotted on radar,
make a run for it.

(Frog avoiding bats)

Hot? Pee on your legs
and stand in the breeze.

(Vulture)

When a member of the group is sick,
slow down to let them catch up.

(Zebra)

With a flasher, it's not the coat you remember
but the white body beneath.

(Grouse)

There's safety in numbers.

(Buffalo)

To sing like a canary,
practice your imitation.

(Bullfinch)

In cars as in birds,
those big fins take a lot of gas.

(Great-tailed grackle)

There is something to be said
for being lazy and stealing.

(Bald eagle)

Healthy, safe, and full? Then play.

(Sea lion)

To be heard in a crowd,
stand in a megaphone.

(Cricket)

If you really want something, whimper.

(Dog)

Despite the noise, the best place to find
a mate is in a crowded meat market.

(Penguin)

CHAPTER TWO

THE BIRDS
AND THE BEES

If you've got no personal means,
attach yourself to a rich victim
and slowly drain the life out of him.

(Virus)

Don't marry someone who smells like you.

(Mouse)

Males may strut,
but females choose their partners.

(Peacock)

If women choose for show,
men will show to extreme.

(Argus pheasant)

Mate for life.

(Snow goose)

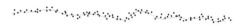

You can lose your head over sex.

(Praying mantis)

When a companion dies,
grieve until the bones are picked clean.

(Pigeon)

To strut your stuff,
you need to be in good shape.

(Sage grouse)

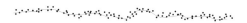

The best aphrodisiac is a little spittle.

(Hermaphrodite slug)

For a good time,
flash your lights five times.

(Glowworm)

When it helps, change your sex.

(Protozoan)

If you're crazy about her,
sing, bow, and jump up and down with joy.

(Sandhill crane)

Night is the time to prowl and howl.

(Hyena)

If you become dependent on someone,
you'll lose your own functions.

(Parasite)

Check which way the wind is blowing
and make your entrance upwind.

(Grizzly bear)

Marry someone with the same colors.

(Goose)

Chocolate, strawberries, a dead fly—
eating in bed is a great aphrodisiac.

(Scorpion fly)

Having an affair can be good for us.

(Ibis are "sneak" copulators)

Here are some new foreplay techniques:
head rubbing, snuffling, snipping,
and snout grabbing.

(Wolf)

Sex can help you make it through
the darkest, stress-filled night.

(Sea anemone)   .

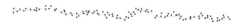

Holding an orgy on the same day every
year can land you in hot water.

(Palolo worm)

You don't need sex that often.
Once every 120 years is plenty
to keep the flower blooming.

(Chinese bamboo)

Sing in harmony, not in unison.

(Wolf)

Don't just jump at that first sniff of sex.
Close your eyes, roll it on your tongue,
check its bouquet for age,
fertility, and willingness.

(Giraffe)

The mating game is rigorous, hurtful,
and sometimes fatal.

(Angel fish)

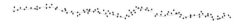

A love song can be your swan song.

(Cricket)

Before prowling at night, take a nap.

(Bat)

If you're desperate to copulate,
splash on the perfume, show your best parts
and walk provocatively.

(Panda)

Foreplay should last days; sex seconds.

(Alligator)

If you want to be polygamous,
you'd better be big and have fat to burn.

(Elephant seal)

Who needs sex?

(80 percent of earth's 30 million species don't)

A little peck on the cheek is a great way
to start an evening together.

(Dove)

Courtship should begin with a duet.

(Sandhill crane)

At high tide,
meet us on the beach for an orgy.

(Grunion)

Marry a man who can fight off predators.

(Zebra)

The more tension between couples,
the stronger the bond.

(Chaffinch)

If you can't feed yourself,
abort your child.

(Rodent)

If a partner dies,
mourn but move on to another.

(Crane)

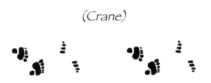

Sex can bond, bribe, and relieve tension.

(Primate)

There are females that
literally "turn on" males.

*(Midshipman fish males flash a light organ when
introduced to a glowing female)*

A personal ad looking for a honey
can attract a bunch of horny losers.

(Frog)

If you've got only one day to mate,
set it on the full moon.

(Sea urchin)

Here's an old line dance: stand together,
wag your heads, flap your arms, preen,
tango, and stick your head in the water.

(Flamingo)

Renounce sex if you wish,
but you'll be boring, predictable,
unadventurous, and often living in exile.

(Dandelion)

Giving sexual favors will keep you well-fed.

(Hummingbird)

Always toast a new friendship.

(Mandarin drakes, upon meeting)

The "better" the female prize,
the more the male will have to fight.

(Elephant seal)

When you're cruising for a mate,
bump bellies and leave a little scent.

(Danaus butterfly)

The more tangled your relationships,
the more complex your songs.

(Polygamous European wren)

Have only as many babies as you can feed.

(Owl)

CHAPTER THREE

LIFE IN THE FAMILY TREE

No matter how long you're married,
don't stop courting.

(Coyote)

If you want your baby to grow to be a
queen, feed her royally.

(Honeybee)

There comes a time in every child's life,
when he's just got to leave home.

(Wolf)

If you're not sure your kids will survive,
have a bunch.

(Rattlesnake)

If someone's trying to steal your child,
offer him sex as a diversion.

(Sea lion)

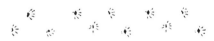

Prepare your children for the cold, cruel world,
but when autumn arrives, drive them out.

(Rodent)

If it's better for the family,
stick around and help raise the kids.

(Lion)

Don't fight with your mother;
you're bound to lose.

(Golden jackal)

Have kids, sure,
but let someone else raise them.

(Cuckoo)

Motherhood is a drag,
so drop the kids and get on with your life.

(Frog)

Don't feel sorry for outcasts;
they're taking the family genes elsewhere.

(Wolf)

When a long-lost family member comes home,
celebrate by screaming, bumping, defecating,
trumpeting, urinating, and stomping around.

(Elephant)

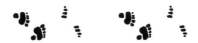

Single moms:
take a companion to protect your children.

(Baboon)

If the man of the house disappears, good
riddance. One of the women can substitute.

(Wrasse fish)

A good watering hole
should be passed on to the kids.

(Sandhill crane)

To raise a healthy and affectionate child,
massage and kiss them all over from birth.

(Cat)

Let the children play—for years.

(Monkey)

If someone's after your kids,
run back and forth shouting "booo!"

(Ostrich)

A super mom pre-chews food
and ingests baby's doo-doo.

(Wolf)

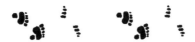

The way you carry yourself, and your place
in the pecking order, is learned as a child.

(Gorilla)

If kids are the goal,
incest may be better than no sex at all.

(Gibbon)

The bigger the brute, the better the father.

(Cichlid fish)

The more a man can help rear the kids,
the more faithful he'll be.

(Beaver)

Once a man has done his duty,
he might as well be food for the kids.

(Insectivorous midge)

If a child is in trouble,
nose him to the surface.

(Dolphin)

An extended family, with uncles,
cousins, and grandparents, is good for kids.

(Florida scrub jay)

When your kid's big enough to feed himself,
chase him up a tree and walk away.

(Grizzly bear)

Take your children to work.

(Rhesus monkey)

The family that plays together stays together.

(Wolf)

Monogamy is good for the kids.

(Over 90 percent of 8,600 species of birds)

After raising your kid, take a year off.

(California condor)

If you've got nasty weapons in the house,
be gentle with your mate.

(Polar bear)

The more babies you have,
the more enemies you'll encounter.

(Bird)

To fool a shark wear a bathing suit
with a dark back and a white belly.

(Killler whale)

Chapter Four
THE WIDE WORLD OF FASHION

Fashion and muscles may cause lust at first sight, but up close it's your smell that counts.

(Butterfly vaalesina)

Never wear white after Easter.

(Ptarmigan)

Flashy clothes attract mates, but they can get you killed too.

(Moth)

Dress up for courting,
but drop the pretension afterward
and get back to work.

(African paradise widowbird)

Girls: forget the fancy clothes;
invest in your family.

(Bird of paradise)

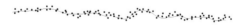

To appear poisonous wear black and yellow.

(Snake)

You'll be left alone if you dress like royalty.

(Viceroy mimicking a Monarch butterfly.)

Ladies, you were born drab
to save your skin and that of your kin.

(Mallard)

The flashier the clothes,
the more assertive the behavior.

(Reef fish)

To avoid getting stung, dress up like a wasp.

(Diptera fly)

To curry favor with a human,
dress like one of his favorites.

(Gold of pleasure plant imitating flax)

Dress like a tasteless cousin
and you'll be avoided.

(Butterfly)

If you're looking to marry,
change into red clothes.

(Three-spined stickleback)

To get the girl, dress to the nines.

(Peacock)

CHAPTER FIVE

ON THE PROWL

Advice for Males ... Of All Species

To get the chick, learn to dance.

(Turkey)

Nothing wins a girl's heart like a small,
sweet treat wrapped in silk.

(Male spider presenting a fly)

When the urge strikes, have sex with
as many females as you can.

(Elk)

Once you find her, never let her go—
even if you go blind.

(Male angler fish attaches to a female, then deteriorates)

Girls respond to breakfast in bed.

(Robin)

Love often takes flight but
some fellows crash and burn.

(Honeybee)

A woman can be lured to your web
by sweet harp music.

(Spider)

When you find your true love,
leap over her and spray her.

(Rabbit)

Some girls just have to be chased.

(Rodent)

Once you've scored,
drop the horns and get back to work.

(Deer)

Testosterone brings out
the best—and worst—in men.

(Humans)

To really impress your girl,
take her on a roller coaster ride,
turn cartwheels, and free-fall
while holding hands.

(Bald eagle)

The guy with the fish gets the gal.

(Kingfisher)

Good vibrations win the girl.

(Water strider)

If it were up to men we'd really have a population problem.

(Human men ejaculate 200 million sperm each time compared to 400 eggs ovulated during a woman's lifetime)

When your wife's vulnerable, guard her.

(Marten in heat)

The more songs you know,
the more women you'll meet.

(Sedge warbler)

Whether you win, lose, or marry
can depend on how well you blow bubbles.

(Humpback whale)

Once you have a female interested,
play hard-to-get by turning your back.

(Peacock)

Foam at the mouth, grind your teeth, and grunt.
You'll stop her in her tracks.

(Boar)

You don't need to strut to win her hand;
hang back, keep your mouth shut,
and sooner or later, she'll come around.

(North American green tree frog)

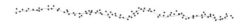

Spray cologne in a corner; it'll keep your
rivals busy while you get the girl.

(Red-sided garter snake)

If you like her looks, grab her hands;
if she struggles a little, let one hand go.
If she struggles a lot, she's not your type.

(Scorpion in mating dance)

Fatal instinct: tie her down first
with silken lines.

(Crab spider)

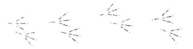

Women love a house filled with junk.

(Bower bird)

They may gawk at muscle-bound guys,
but many females prefer average Joes.

(Elk)

A good roar is irresistible to women.

(Crocodile)

When calling on a lady friend,
knock before entering.

(Tortoise)

If you don't have the muscle to
mate like the big boys,
try sneaking around.

(Salamander)

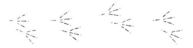

Tell your honey you're all eyes for her.

(Peacock)

Advice for Females ... Of All Species

You can never have too many men.

(Wattled jacana)

The showier the man,
the more likely he is to wander.

(Bird of paradise)

Who needs men
when you've got parthenogenesis?

(Goldfish)

A male gathering is a good place
to look them over.

(Cicada in trees)

Men are expendable.

(Lizard)

The longer the courtship, the greater the
chance the guy will hang around.

(Red-necked phalarope)

There's nothing like a mud bath
to make you feel like a new woman.

(Hippopotamus)

A young woman is less likely to marry
if Dad is still around.

(Prairie dog)

No wonder she killed him; he was
beating her about the head during sex.

(Praying mantis)

The deeper the voice,
the older and wiser the guy.

(North American tree frog)

Hunks can rule for a year or two,
but they soon get pushed aside.

(Elephant seal)

In an otherwise dangerous world,
a sorority is a sweet, serene spot.

(Honeybee)

The scent of a woman—
use it to catch a man.

(Channel catfish)

When being courted,
stay as long as the food lasts.

(Scorpion fly female)

Don't settle for the flashiest hunk;
make sure he'll support you
and your family.

(Bee-eater)

Men will risk their lives for a lady.

(Hanging fly)

If you're not interested in sex,
whack his penis with your flipper.

(Elephant seal)

Judge your man on his ability to feed you.

(Common tern)

If your guy didn't feed you well last year,
drop him.

(Red-billed gull)

Double your weight before winter.

(Ground squirrel)

CHAPTER SIX

FEEDING FRENZY

You can jump on anything that moves,
but YOU may get eaten in the process.

(Bee)

If you're hungry and not getting fed,
push your siblings out of the house.

(Egret)

If you're REALLY hungry, eat yourself.

(Sea anemone)

There's no such thing as a free lunch;
when the food's gone, leave or perish.

(Hawk)

There will be more food for you if you drag
your weak brother around the house, bite
and harass him until he dies of exhaustion.

(Bald eagle)

You can raid the refrigerator
if you're a maid.

(Cleaning fish)

A hungry child can get fed
by imitating somebody else's kid.

(Widow bird)

You can live very well on leftovers.

(Hyena)

In the dark, beware the lighted bait.

(Angler fish)

When hungry,
steal food off someone else's plate.

(Bald eagle)

Spend your summer
burying seeds for the winter.

(Ground squirrel)

If a stranger happens by,
gobble up the food before he can eat it.

(Dog)

Sometimes you've got to
eat garbage to survive.

(Seagull)

For a good meal,
watch where the crowd's going.

(Ferruginous hawk)

If you didn't get all the vitamins the first time,
eat your poop.

(Rabbit)

Dropping in during dinnertime
usually gets you fed.

(Eagle)

When you find a good restaurant,
dance the directions to your buddies.

(Honeybee)

Take slaves to gather food.

(Ant)

Eat only when you're hungry.

(Cat)

A deep bass will scare off
a squeaky alto every time.

(Common toad)

CHAPTER SEVEN
SURVIVAL OF THE FITTEST

A street gang is more likely to kill
than a loner.

(Wolf)

A female can drive males to fight.

(Mallard)

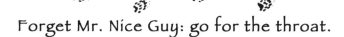

Forget Mr. Nice Guy: go for the throat.

(Wolverine)

When you're in big trouble, play dead.

(Spider)

You can bluff only once.

(Wolf)

When you see you're licked, roll over,
tuck your tail, and whine.

(Red fox)

You can scare a competitor
just by staring them down.

(Panda)

Sometimes you've just got to
knock heads with a rival.

(Turtle)

Small? Use the element of surprise.

(Fox)

Mob an enemy.

(Starling)

It's dangerous to fight.
Better to beat your chest and threaten.

(Gorilla)

Without the home court advantage,
you'll probably lose.

(Many species)

If you see trouble coming, crow,
puff up, and stomp around.

(Rooster)

Fight for three things: territory, a mate,
and your kids. All else is destructive.

(Wolf)

If you advertise yourself too loudly,
your enemy will find you, too.

(Male cricket)

Don't get mad, get even.

(Primate)

Even a pint-sized opponent
bristles with confidence
when defending his home.

(Cichlid fish)

If you know you're a wimp, don't try puffing up; find another way to do business.

(Monkey)

If attacked, throw your guts up.

(Sea cucumber,
which grows a new digestive tract)

If you're about to get spanked, pretend you're already hurt.

(Dog)

If you haven't got the will to fight,
change your spots.

(Chameleon)

If a comrade falls,
carry him off the battlefield.

(Elephant)

If you're being pursued,
leave your tail behind.

(Skink)

Top dogs keep the young bucks at bay
by flashing big, toothy grins.

(Wolf)

In bar fights, it is far better
to kill the spirit than the body.

(Ram)

Check his weapon before you knock heads.

(Deer)

Before you enter the swamp,
size up the rivals by listening carefully.

(Toad)

The smell of death, like the smell of money,
attracts slimy, crawly things.

(Southern pine bark beetle)

Before going in for the kill,
test your prey for weaknesses.

(Wolf pack)

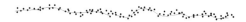

Smart men don't risk injury;
they play games to determine the winner.

(Viper)

If assaulted by a bigger male,
act like you're a female.

(Sea lion)

Follow the leader.
Let the strongest take the risk.

(Baboon)

A female can raise her rank in a clan
by marrying a dominant male.

(Monkey)

Run yourself ragged on the job,
and you'll get beaten by a competitor.

(Rabbit)

CHAPTER EIGHT

THE RAT RACE

Remember in business as in life,
the slow, sick, and unaware die first.

(Moose)

To appear important at a power lunch,
deepen your voice.

(Frog)

Expect to score a killer deal
only one time in four.

(Coyote)

Call a meeting with perfume.

(Slime mold)

To hone your job skills, make them a game.

(Lion)

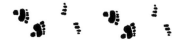

When all else fails with the boss,
try bribing him with a banana.

(Chimpanzee)

In a business or clan,
stress attacks the high and low ranks.
You live longer in middle management.

(Monkey)

The office pecking order
doesn't require real claws. Posture, play,
and a bit of arm wrestling is all it takes.

(Panda)

Advertising must be honest
and claims backed up.

(Bighorn sheep)

No one will mess with you
if you sleep in a dangerous place.

(Clown fish in sea anemone)

CHAPTER NINE

A HOME ON
THE RANGE

Don't put roots down if you can't thrive.
Wait for rain and better times.

(Rose of Jericho)

Scatter thorns to keep
snakes out of the house.

(African weaver)

Every day, pick up the house, take a bath,
and check your partner for lice.

(Primate)

Once you build a home,
keep it in the family for 400 years.

(Stork)

If you must build in a flood plain,
make sure your house floats.

(Duck)

What a wonderful world it would be
if territory were seized by song.

(White-throated sparrow)

If things get really crowded at home,
head for the shore.

(Lemming)

To claim a homesite,
sing and dab a little musk on the corners.

(Elk)

When your house needs cleaning,
rely on a professional.

(Sea swallow)

There's nothing like a good ol' fashioned
hysterical mob to drive an unwanted
out of your neighborhood.

(Songbird)

When you've got your new home done,
puff your chest, roll your eyes,
and cry "gaa, aah aah aah."

(Penguin)

The guy with the best house
gets the most dates.

(Yellow-bellied marmot)

You know what they always say about home real estate: location (food), location (water), and location (protection).

(Zebra)

ABOUT THE AUTHORS

Jim Carrier, a roaming western columnist for the *Denver Post*, has been a journalist for 30 years. He traces his interest in the natural world to his childhood on a farm in upstate New York. Since 1984 Carrier has covered the Rocky Mountains for the *Denver Post*. Notable natural history projects included a four-month series in Yellowstone National Park, "Letters from Yellowstone," and a three-month journey on the Colorado River. Carrier has also published six books on western issues. Prior to moving to Colorado, Carrier built an earth-sheltered, passive solar, off-the-electric grid home in the Black Hills of South Dakota, where he practiced living with nature.

Marc Bekoff is a professor in the Department of Environmental, Population, and Organismic Biology at the University of Colorado, Boulder. A Fellow of the Animal Behavior Society and a Guggenheim Fellow, he has conducted research on the social behavior of various canids, including coyotes, wolves, and domestic dogs; adélie penguins in Antarctica; and various species of birds living in the Front Range of Colorado. His major interests are concerned with the evolution and development of social behavior and animal cognition or thinking. He also spends a lot of time thinking and writing about animal welfare.